Brands We Know

Apple

By Sara Green

Bellwether Media • Minneapolis, MN

Jump into the cockpit and take flight with Pilot books. Your journey will take you on high-energy adventures as you learn about all that is wild, weird, fascinating, and fun!

This edition first published in 2016 by Bellwether Media, Inc.

No part of this publication may be reproduced in whole or in part without written permission of the publisher.
For information regarding permission, write to Bellwether Media, Inc.,
Attention: Permissions Department,
5357 Penn Avenue South, Minneapolis, MN 55419.

Library of Congress Cataloging-in-Publication Data

Green, Sara, 1964- author.
 Apple / by Sara Green.
   pages cm. -- (Pilot. Brands We Know)
 Summary: "Engaging images accompany information about Apple,
Inc. The combination of high-interest subject matter and narrative text
is intended for students in grades 3 through 7"-- Provided by publisher.
 Audience: Ages 7-12
 Audience: Grades 3 to 7
 Includes bibliographical references and index.
 ISBN 978-1-62617-286-9 (hardcover: alk. paper)
1. Apple Computer, Inc.--Juvenile literature. 2. Computer industry--
United States--Juvenile literature. I. Title.
 HD9696.2.U64A67336 2016
 338.7'61004160973--dc23
                          2015002649

Printed in the United States of America, North Mankato, MN.

Table of Contents

What Is Apple?

Every day, people across the globe use Apple products. They listen to music, send text messages, and browse the Internet. Most people are familiar with the company's apple-shaped **logo**. In 2015, Apple Inc. was worth more than $740 billion. This makes it the most valuable **brand** on Earth!

Apple Inc., also known as Apple, strives to make **innovative** products that are stylish and easy to use. The company **headquarters** is in Cupertino, California. Apple is best known for its Macintosh computers, iPods, iPhones, and iPads. It also makes computer **software** and other electronic devices. All Apple products easily connect to one another. Today, many people cannot imagine a life without Apple technology.

By the Numbers

more than
90,000
employees
worldwide in 2014

more than
25 billion
songs sold
on iTunes

more than
1.4 million
apps available
from App Store

16
countries with
Apple retail stores

more than
200 million
iPads sold since 2010

Apple headquarters

How Apple Began

Apple began in 1976 with two men named Steve. Steve Jobs and Steve Wozniak, also known as Woz, shared an interest in computers. At that time, few people owned computers. Most were so large that one would fill an entire room. Woz had a plan for a smaller computer. It would make computers easier to buy and to use. Steve Jobs saw a big opportunity. People could use these computers at home, school, or the office. He convinced Woz to start a computer business with him. They called it Apple Computer, Inc. Woz was responsible for inventing products. Steve was in charge of selling them.

In 1976, Woz built the company's first personal computer. It was called the Apple I. This computer was just a **circuit board**. It had no case, keyboard, or monitor. Working out of Steve's family garage, a small team made 50 Apple I computers within a month. All the computers sold. Steve and Woz were thrilled with their success.

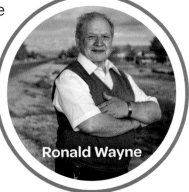

Ronald Wayne

No Regrets

Ronald Wayne was another company founder who left after just 12 days. He sold his share of Apple Computer, Inc. for $800. Today, it would have been worth billions.

Byte into an Apple

1970s Apple Computer tagline

Steve Jobs

Steve Wozniak

7

Woz began to design a better computer. In 1977, he introduced the Apple II. It had a keyboard and capability for color **graphics**. This grew the company even more. By 1980, Apple sales reached $117 million. Steve and Woz were millionaires!

Apple Computer was achieving success, but Woz did not enjoy running the company. He continued at Apple, but he shifted his focus to activities outside it. Steve then hired a man named John Sculley to lead Apple.

John Sculley

Apple II

The power to be your best.
1980s-1990s Apple Computer tagline

.... **Macintosh computer**

A Favorite Apple
The name Macintosh is based on a variety of apple called the McIntosh.

In 1984, Apple made history. That year, the company introduced the Macintosh computer, also known as the Mac. It included **icons** and a mouse to control the desktop. These made using a computer much easier than ever before. They would become a new standard for personal computers. However, Steve and John disagreed about how to run the company. In 1985, Steve left Apple to start a new computer company called NeXT, Inc. By this time, Woz had also **resigned**. The company's **founders** were gone, but Apple continued to move forward.

Moving Forward

Apple introduced the PowerBook in 1991. This laptop computer was the first of many models in the line. Each new PowerBook was faster and sleeker than the one before. PowerBooks were popular, but Apple faced new problems. Other computer companies such as Microsoft were making products similar to Apple's. They sold them in more places at lower prices. In the mid-1990s, Apple saw a drop in sales. The company needed a new plan.

Steve and NeXT helped rescue Apple. In 1996, Apple bought NeXT. It used NeXT's software and powerful **operating system** to design better computers. In time, Apple's **board of directors** asked Steve to lead the company again. He agreed. Steve made many changes, including limiting the products Apple made. These changes got the company back on track. In 1998, Apple released a new computer called the iMac. This colorful computer was a hit with customers. It soon became one of the best-selling personal computers in the United States.

The Apple Of My i
The "i" in Apple product names stands for Internet.

Hello. Again.
1990s iMac tagline

The 2000s brought more changes to the company. Apple began to shift its focus to mobile electronic devices. These would become Apple's top products. In 2001, the company released a small digital music player called the iPod. The first iPods could store 1,000 songs. Over time, Apple improved the iPod's design and storage. Today's iPods can store up to 15,000 songs.

2001 iPod

2014 iPod Touch

Apple TV

Apple TV is a device that sits on television sets. It allows people to stream shows, movies, videos, and sports from the Internet to their televisions.

Apple TV

iTunes Store

iTunes
gift cards

iTunes U

In 2001, Apple also introduced a program called iTunes. It played and organized music. In 2003, Apple launched the iTunes Music Store. This allowed people to buy music, too. Today, the iTunes Store also carries movies, television shows, e-books, **podcasts**, and **apps**. It offers more than 43 million songs and 85,000 movies! People can also take lessons through iTunes U. This program offers online educational classes for students of all ages. Some school classrooms use iTunes U. Students download assignments and other materials on mobile devices or computers. This allows them to study and learn anywhere.

Imagining Possibilities

The success of Apple's mobile devices led to another change. The name "Apple Computer" no longer fit the products. In 2007, Steve renamed the company Apple Inc. That year, Apple released the iPhone. It was one of the first phones with a touch screen. Apple has since made the iPhone faster and given it more storage. It also has a better camera and sharper display. Apple introduced a **tablet** computer called the iPad in 2010. It was an instant hit! People can check email, download apps, watch videos, and read e-books on its larger touch screen.

iPhone

iPad .....

This changes everything. Again.

2010s iPhone 4 tagline

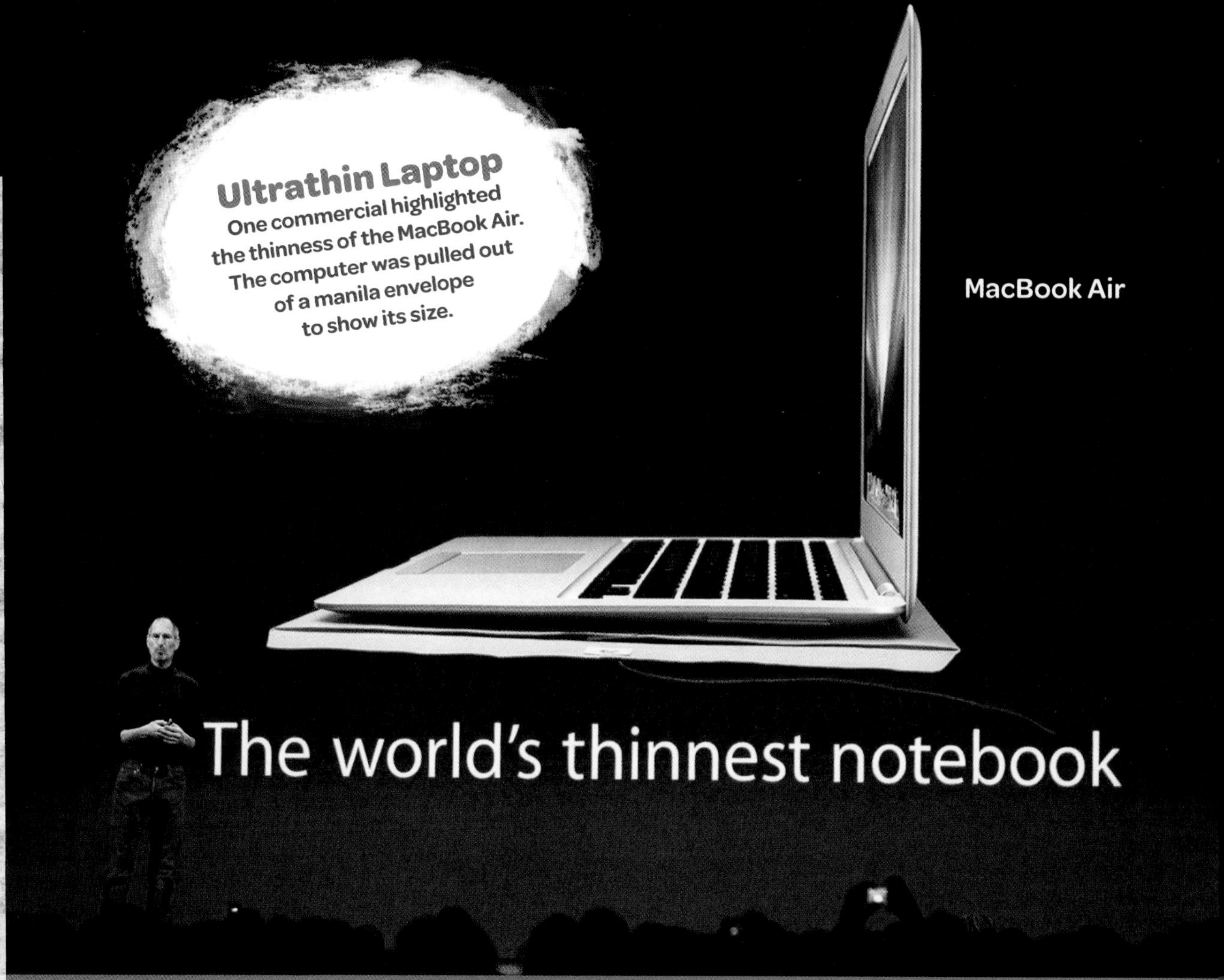

MacBook Air

The world's thinnest notebook

Apple has become famous for its clever **advertising** as well as its innovative products. Early iPod commercials attracted attention for their bright colors and catchy songs. Other ads show people using Apple products in creative ways. One iPad commercial shows how the device helps a deaf woman explore the world. Apple's imaginative ads continue to reflect its groundbreaking products.

Sadly, Steve Jobs passed away in 2011. However, the company remains true to his vision. Apple continues to create innovative products that people love to use. One new service is called Apple Pay. People use a mobile Apple device to pay for purchases instead of credit cards. They hold their device up to electronic readers. Then the amount is automatically billed to their credit card.

The Apple Watch is also new. This computer fits on the wrist. It has a full-color screen and offers a variety of apps. Apple Watches help users track health information, send messages, and keep time.

Apple continues to make improvements to many of its products. The iPhone 6 has two body sizes. A future version may offer a third, smaller one. It could also have a 3D display! However, Apple keeps future products secret. Until they are released, people can only guess what Apple will come up with next.

....

A Huge Deal

In 2014, Apple bought Beats Music and Beats Electronics for $3 billion. The company provides a music streaming service to paying customers. It also makes top-quality headphones and speakers.

Apple Products
By Year Released

1976	Apple I
1977	Apple II
1983	Apple IIe
1984	Macintosh
1986	Macintosh Plus
1987	Macintosh II
1991	Macintosh PowerBook
1998	iMac
1999	iBook
2001	iPod
2004	iPod Mini
2005	iPod Shuffle
2006	MacBook Pro
2007	Apple TV
2007	iPhone
2008	MacBook Air
2010	iPad
2014	iPhone 6
2015	Apple Watch

Helping Others

Apple helps make a difference in people's lives in other ways. The company donated $50 million to Stanford University's hospitals. It has also donated more than $100 million to (RED). This organization is dedicated to ending **AIDS** in Africa. Apple released special (PRODUCT) RED items to support the organization.

Apple employees also play an important role in giving. When employees donate money to **charities**, Apple matches each donation up to $10,000. This has raised more than $50 million since the program began in 2011. Apple also donates to charities where Apple employees **volunteer**. The charities receive $25 for every hour an employee volunteers there.

Apple even helps **victims** of natural disasters. It uses the iTunes Store to collect donations for them. In 2012, the company donated $2.5 million to help victims of **Hurricane** Sandy. Through technology and donations, Apple helps improve the lives of many people.

Change is
in the Air.

2010s iPad Air 2 tagline

Apple Timeline

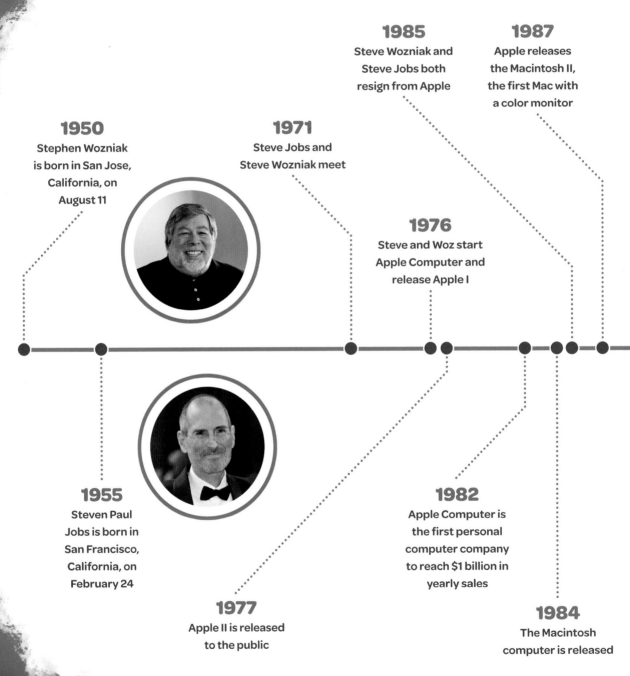

1950
Stephen Wozniak is born in San Jose, California, on August 11

1955
Steven Paul Jobs is born in San Francisco, California, on February 24

1971
Steve Jobs and Steve Wozniak meet

1977
Apple II is released to the public

1976
Steve and Woz start Apple Computer and release Apple I

1985
Steve Wozniak and Steve Jobs both resign from Apple

1982
Apple Computer is the first personal computer company to reach $1 billion in yearly sales

1987
Apple releases the Macintosh II, the first Mac with a color monitor

1984
The Macintosh computer is released

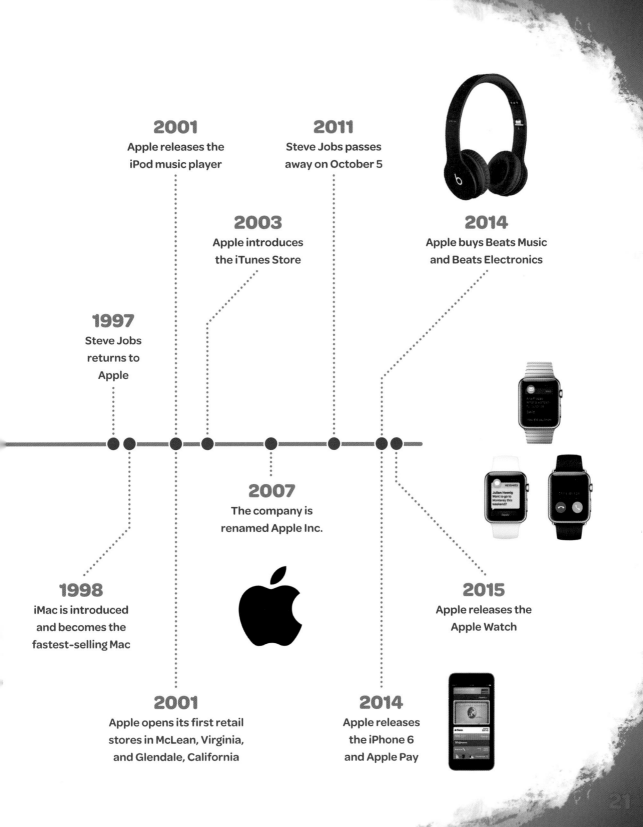

2001
Apple releases the
iPod music player

2011
Steve Jobs passes
away on October 5

2003
Apple introduces
the iTunes Store

2014
Apple buys Beats Music
and Beats Electronics

1997
Steve Jobs
returns to
Apple

2007
The company is
renamed Apple Inc.

1998
iMac is introduced
and becomes the
fastest-selling Mac

2015
Apple releases the
Apple Watch

2001
Apple opens its first retail
stores in McLean, Virginia,
and Glendale, California

2014
Apple releases
the iPhone 6
and Apple Pay

Glossary

advertising—notices and messages that announce or promote something

AIDS—a serious disease of the immune system; AIDS stands for Acquired Immunodeficiency Syndrome.

apps—small, specialized programs downloaded onto smartphones and other mobile devices

board of directors—a group of people who oversee the activities of a company or organization

brand—a category of products all made by the same company

charities—organizations that help others in need

circuit board—a thin plate where chips and other electronic parts are attached

founders—the people who created a company

graphics—art such as illustrations or designs

headquarters—a company's main office

hurricane—a spinning rainstorm that starts over warm waters

icons—small pictures on a computer screen that represent a program or function

innovative—introducing new ideas and methods

logo—a symbol or design that identifies a brand or product

operating system—the main program in a computer that controls the way it works; an operating system makes it possible for other computer programs to function.

podcasts—talk or music programs that can be downloaded onto a computer or mobile device

resigned—left a position

software—a program that tells a computer what to do

tablet—a handheld computer

victims—people in need of help

volunteer—to do something for others without expecting money in return

To Learn More

AT THE LIBRARY

Gilbert, Sara. *Built for Success: The Story of Apple.* Mankato, Minn.: Creative Education, 2011.

Goldsmith, Mike, and Tom Jackson. *Computer.* New York, N.Y.: DK Publishing, 2011.

Green, Sara. *Steve Jobs.* Minneapolis, Minn.: Bellwether Media, 2015.

ON THE WEB

Learning more about Apple is as easy as 1, 2, 3.

1. Go to www.factsurfer.com.

2. Enter "Apple" into the search box.

3. Click the "Surf" button and you will see a list of related web sites.

With factsurfer.com, finding more information is just a click away.

Index